I am thirteen years old.
I like the subject English.
I am the first black president of America.

LES BONS SAMARITAINS

COLLEGE
JAMES M.ST

Printed and bound in the United States of America

ISBN: 978-0-9858898-0-7

 Medinger Media Press
P.O. Box 1529
Ellicott City, MD 21041

Publisher: Daniel L. Medinger
Project Manager: Megan M. Purpora
Designer: Erin A. Heilman

When I Was In Haiti
Stories of Hope from Travelers

Medinger Media Press
www.medingermedia.com

This book is dedicated to two of my best friends, Cardinal William H. Keeler and the late Bishop Emmanuel Constant without whose constant advice and encouragement this book would not exist.

ACKNOWLEDGEMENTS

Thank you to all of the bloggers and photographers,
especially those included in this book:

Anebi Adoga, Jr.
Rachel Barron
Patrick Brady
Ellen Bundy
Becca Dean
Allie Dillon
Judy Dillon
Laikyn Duffey
Diane and Dave
    Dugan
Danielle Freiji
Laura Goudreau
Willis Gunther
Abby Hill
Anthony Hutcherson

Philippe Jallon
Caitlin Jones
Lauren Kelly
Kate Lagna
Arnie Landers
John Lear
Timothy Lear
Dr. Lewis Libby III
Sarah Malishchack
Emily Mastin
Kathy Mayer
Missy Mazzullo
Daniel Medinger
Denise Mitchell
Cristina Mollenkopf

Sarah Morsheimer
Cecile Mortel
Dr. Kevin Murphy
John O'Donnell
Marc Parisi
Hannah Patten
Marvin Roxas
Agnes and Charles
    Supernavage
Dr. Jim Taneyhill
Dolores and Rich
    Tibbets
Rick Ulrich

A special thank you to all sponsors and supporters, especially:

Cardinal William H. Keeler

Cardinal Edwin F. O'Brien

Food for the Poor, Inc.

Archdiocese of Baltimore

The Horatio Alger Association of
    Distinguished Americans, Inc.

Cortopassi Family Foundation

James M. and Margaret V. Stine
    Foundation

United Food and Commercial
    Workers International Union

Patten Family Foundation

Samuel W. Chairs Jr.

When I Was In Haiti

Stories of Hope from Travelers

HOW TO READ THIS BOOK

This book shares the stories of those who have visited the schools in Haiti. It includes observations of Dr. Rod Mortel, who founded the schools. It also includes photos of the people, activities and facilities sponsored by the Mortel Family Charitable Foundation. While some may choose to read the book "cover to cover," each page can individually tell the story and success of this hopeful mission.

TABLE OF CONTENTS

PREFACE

The Mortel Family Charitable Foundation serves economically, socially and intellectually deprived children and adults of Haiti.

For more than a decade, we have planted seeds of hope by building schools and providing meals and health care to children. We also offer opportunities for adult literacy and vocational training.

Yes, it is a challenging mission to work in St. Marc, a bustling community about 50 miles north of Port-au-Prince. But where some people see poverty and despair, we see hope and opportunity. We see the loving face of Jesus in every child. The Mortel Family Charitable Foundation offers the opportunity to share this special beauty of Haiti with others by way of student sponsorships, exchange programs and special visitations. Every person who has visited Good Samaritans School (Les Bons Samaritains) or James Stine College (College James M. Stine) in St. Marc has returned with gifts that can only come from meeting the Haitian people face to face. Please note that for readability the schools are referenced by their English translation (i.e. Good Samaritans School and James Stine College)throughout the book.

Our mission, succinctly put, is to "empower through education." For our students, we want them to see and feel the benefits of this empowerment each day. For those who have traveled to Haiti with the Mortel Family Charitable Foundation, we want them to witness how they can be empowered by learning more about our brothers and sisters in Haiti. Now, you, the reader, are invited to enter into this opportunity to be empowered with the knowledge, faith and hope that comes from Haiti.

Some of the stories here will bring smiles and others a sigh. But each story and photo is a testimony to the power of love and the strength of commitment needed to change the future of Haiti one child at a time.

Those who support and collaborate with the Mortel Family Charitable Foundation are helping to shape a brighter future for Haiti. This book is a testament to the hopeful enterprise of these schools.

DR. RODRIGUE MORTEL

"I know what it is to be poor, hungry and have no hope.

I traveled down that road."

– *Rodrigue Mortel*

DR. RODRIGUE MORTEL

A Humbling Childhood

Dr. Rodrigue Mortel was born and educated in Haiti. He was only one of a multitude of children growing up in the overpopulated, impoverished Haiti in the 1930s. He was born into abject poverty, in a small rented house of wattle and daub, lacking even the minimal necessities of water and electricity. When they were evicted from this meanest of dwellings because his parents could not pay the monthly rent of $4, young Rodrigue vowed such an indignity would never again be permitted against his family.

"This would not have happened if I had been educated," his mother acknowledged. The words his mother spoke were permanently etched in his heart as he silently pledged that he would finish his education and someday build a house for his mother. He could not have known that he was destined to accomplish much more for his family and country.

Rodrigue dedicated himself to moving his way through Haiti's highly competitive public education program. He understood that a superior education would arm him with the tools he needed to make a better life for himself and his family.

Fighting Against All Odds

He practiced general medicine for two years in rural Haiti following his graduation from the Medical School of Port-au-Prince. Then, he spent one year of graduate study in Montreal before entering the United States in 1963. Dr. Mortel received training in the field of obstetrics and gynecology at the Hahnemann Medical College and Hospital in Philadelphia and then sub-specialized in gynecologic oncology at the Memorial Sloan Kettering Cancer Center in New York City.

Subsequently, he joined the Penn State University College of Medicine in 1972 as an assistant professor and quickly climbed the academic ladder to become a full professor in the Department of Obstetrics and Gynecology in 1977. Six years later, he became the first black foreign educated chairman of one of the 126 U.S. medical schools' departments of obstetrics and gynecology. He held this position for nearly 13 years before his promotion in 1995 to associate dean and founding director of the Penn State University Cancer Center.

He was always recognized as one of the best teachers at Penn State and consequently received outstanding performance evaluations by medical students, residents and fellows. His reputation as one of the best cancer surgeons has crossed over the borders of Pennsylvania to reach the entire United States as well as European and Asian countries. That was confirmed in 1993 and 1997 when Dr. Mortel was named one of the Best 401 Doctors for Women in the United States.

Returning to His Roots

Dr. Mortel remains deeply rooted in Haiti. He returns numerous times every year to volunteer his time and services to hospitals there. He was one of the two Haitians chosen to serve on the long range planning committee for the Albert Schweitzer Hospital in Haiti. Dr. Mortel's international experience extends beyond Haiti. For example, he went to Romania to assess health care needs of the population and in past years donated medical and surgical supplies, diagnostic x-ray equipment, hospital beds and office furnishings to Romanian hospitals, in addition to the Haitian hospitals he helped support.

In 1997, he founded The Mortel Family Charitable Foundation, a 501(c)3 organization incorporated in Pennsylvania. *High Hopes for Haiti* is sponsored by The Mortel Family Charitable Foundation and is the continuing program that connects the people of Haiti to supporters of the Foundation. The mission of the Foundation is to serve the economically, socially and intellectually deprived people of Haiti. Having determined that empowering people with education is the most effective means to achieve a self-sufficient and productive life, the Foundation establishes, operates and maintains a variety of educational programs.

The Foundation is responsible for the operational costs of Good Samaritans School, an elementary school, and oversees operations of a secondary school, James Stine College, which opened its doors in the Fall, 2011, in St. Marc, Haiti. This high school provides secondary education especially to the graduates of the Good Samaritans School.

Dr. Mortel also opened the Cardinal Keeler Center, a vocational school which provides Haitians the opportunity to acquire technical skills in various trades including plumbing, electricity, carpentry, auto mechanics, masonry, craftsmanship, sewing and so on. The inaugural class entered the school in September, 2007, consisting of adolescents from both the Gonaives and St. Marc regions.

Compassionate Healer

Dr. Mortel is also a scientist. After studying in one of the best cancer research laboratories at the University of Paris, he became a fellow of the Ligue Nationale Francaise contre le Cancer, conducted extensive research in his laboratory at Penn State and developed a new method of treating women with cancer of the uterus, which he shared with the medical academic community.

In 1988, Dr. Mortel competed successfully to be one of the six Robert Wood Johnson Health Policy Fellows selected by the Institute of Medicine of the National Academy of Sciences. He served for one year as a health aide to Congressman Sander Levin of the Health Subcommittee of the House Committee on Ways and Means. He has been a member of the advisory board of the National Cancer Institute from 1979 to 2000 and served as legislative watchdog for the Society of Gynecologic Oncologists while he led the Society's efforts to establish a gynecologic oncology section within the National Cancer Institute.

Dr. Mortel has published two books, 135 articles and chapters in books, as well as editorials in various periodicals including *The New York Times* and *The Washington Post.* For his numerous achievements, Dr. Mortel has received many awards and occupied leadership positions in all prestigious obstetrical and gynecological societies in the United States and Haiti. He received the U.S. Public Health Service Award in 1970; the prestigious Horatio Alger Award in 1985 (From Rags to Riches); and the highly coveted Faculty Scholar Medal from Penn State for outstanding achievement in the area of health sciences in 1986. He is the creator and founding chairman of the Gynecologic Cancer Foundation (GCF) and became, in 1994, the first foreigner to be president of the elite American Society of Gynecologic Oncologists (SGO).

Fighting for the Future

Since 1986, Dr. Mortel has become a motivational speaker to high school students, a keynote speaker at college graduation ceremonies, has appeared on Robert Schuller's television program "Hour of Power" and received the Churchman of the Year Award in 1991. Dr. Mortel was the recipient in 1997 of the Award for Excellence in Education and Health from the National Organization for the Advancement of Haitians (NOAH). In May, 1999, he received an award from the Haitian Institute for outstanding achievement in medicine, education and research. In January, 2000, he received the "Doctor of the Decade" award, the most prestigious award of the South Florida Chapter of the Association of Haitian Physicians Abroad. On May 18, 2002, Dr. Mortel received "The Drs. Kienle's Humanistic Medicine" award from Penn State College of Medicine for demonstrating the highest standards in dealing with patients, colleagues and the community.

Dr. Mortel retired from the medical field and is currently serving as a Roman Catholic permanent deacon, with many irons in the fire of ministry. He entered a diaconate formation program in 1998, studied for three years in Baltimore and was ordained on July 5, 2011, incardinated in the Diocese of Gonaives, Haiti.

He heads the Missions Office for the Archdiocese of Baltimore, furthering the church's missionary work around the world. He runs the Baltimore-Haiti Project, a program for Baltimore Archdiocesan Catholics to spiritually and materially help the poorest of the poor in Haiti. All of these organizations are separate, yet all are blessed by the services of Dr. Mortel.

The Mortel Family Charitable Foundation

One of the goals of The Mortel Family Charitable Foundation is to connect the beauty of Haiti with missionaries from the United States. To accomplish this initiative, a visiting program was established to allow youth and adults the opportunity to experience Haiti.

Travelers come to Haiti, volunteering their time and services to improve the living conditions in the Diocese of Gonaives, but in return they experience a life-changing event by working side-by-side with Haitian students.

Those who travel to Good Samaritans School and James Stine College learn first-hand the needs and the successes of this amazing Foundation.

The visiting program has an enormous impact.

Denise (Mortel) Mitchell, Cecile Mortel, Dr. Rod Mortel and Reneé (Mortel) Joy

Visitors gain knowledge and experience a world outside of their own. They are immersed in Haiti with its rampant poverty, but filled with people of hope, pride, faith and love in their hearts. It is something to witness.

The Mortel Family Charitable Foundation builds awareness and empowers through education.

www.mortelfoundation.org
www.highhopesforhaiti.org
www.goodsamaritansschool.org
www.jamesstinecollege.org

HAITI

HISTORY IN BRIEF

The native Taino Amerindians – who inhabited the island of Hispaniola when it was discovered by Christopher Columbus in 1492 – were virtually annihilated by Spanish settlers within 25 years. In the early 17th century, the French established a presence on Hispaniola. In 1697, Spain ceded to the French the western third of the island, which later became Haiti. The French colony, based on forestry and sugar-related industries, became one of the wealthiest in the Caribbean, but only through the heavy importation of African slaves and considerable environmental degradation. In the late 18th century, Haiti's nearly half million slaves revolted under Toussaint Louverture. After a prolonged struggle, Haiti became the first black republic in the western hemisphere to declare independence in 1804. It wasn't until 2006 that Haiti inaugurated a democratically elected president and parliament.

HAITI QUICK FACTS

Capital:	Port-au-Prince
Independence:	January 1, 1804 *(from France)*
Total Size:	10,715 sq. miles
Distance from US:	700 miles approx.
Population:	9,801,664
Currency:	Haitian gourde
Languages:	French (official), Creole (official)
Religions:	80% Roman Catholic, 16% Protestant, 1% none, 3% other
Infant Mortality Rate:	52.44 deaths/1,000 live births
Life Expectancy:	62.51 years
Literacy:	52.9% are literate
People below poverty line:	80%
Average Income:	2$/day approx. $730 annually

THE HAITIAN FLAG

The Haitian flag is comprised of two equal horizontal bands of blue and red with a centered white rectangle bearing the coat of arms, which contains a palm tree

flanked by flags and two cannons above a scroll bearing the motto, L'union Fait La Force (Union Makes Strength); the colors are taken from the French Tricolor and represent the union of blacks and mulattoes.

HAITI

In St. Marc, Haiti, two schools willed into being by Dr. Rod Mortel are impacting the present and changing the future of how people view Haiti. The power of faith, the deep-rooted culture and the determination of Haitians to make their country better, is what travelers to the community and school see each day.

The school... from previous... trembler was ab... screaming in the... learning more about the... rooms and the building held up... making it about the size of the state of Maryland. Located in the Caribbean Sea, it is 565 miles Southeast of Florid... these mountains used to be covered with lush green forest, but now few trees r... Over the past few decades ex... y more children now compared to 7 years ago. I wondered how the... **Haiti is a** ...rthquake and what their li... nd wiser! I was informed by phone that Good Samaritan Sc...**ated in the Caribbean S**...e school children were ...**ainous**...earthquake and the after shocks were felt in St. Marc. ...**ntains used to be covered with**... I heard about the ...i look mu...e bleeding. So many... **school has**...**every year, and there are so many mo**... following state...e. When I got...thquake...eir smiles and joy were same as I remembered from previous summer...the isl...ool children were "okay" after the devastating earthquake that shook Haiti. The epicenter of the ...arc. I was on the phone immediately after I heard about...rthquake and I spoke with people i...had just returned from Haiti, a d...the earth...just missin...e following staten...arthquake in Haiti, our hearts are bl...man...ds are suffering s...Word from St ...ms and the building held up." As everyo...Haiti is only 11,000 square miles making...the sta...Maryla...ed in the...ically, the island is very mountain...coas...to be...red in these forests making Hai...ok much...ean,...th...d what their lives were now like. When I g...t...les...joy we...membe...ool in St. Marc, Haiti, and the school child...e "o...er th...vast...art...e that s...after shocks were felt in St. Marc. I was o...hone...iately...er...ea...about...arthqua...ld that the school was okay."I had just ret...from...a day b...ore the...hqua...it, just m...ore about the devastating earthquake in H...ur hea...re bleeding. So m...friend...are sufferi...ildren calm in their classrooms and the buil...q held...s everyone kno...rom the tragic earth...the Dominican Republic. Haiti is only 11,000 square mi...aking it about...size of the state of...million people. Geographically, the island is very moun...s with flat...along its coasts. T...ensive logging has occurred in these forests making H...k much li...sert. The school has...survived the earthquake and what their lives were no...hen I go...their smiles and joy

HAITI IS...

Haiti is a small country on the island of Hispaniola and it shares the island with its neighbor the Dominican Republic.

Haiti is only 10,715 square miles, making it about the size of the state of Maryland. Located in the Caribbean Sea, it is 700 miles southeast of Florida. It has a population of nearly 10 million people. Geographically, the island is very mountainous with flat plains along its coasts. The mountains used to be covered with lush green forest, but now few trees remain. Decades of extensive logging makes Haiti look like a desert.

The school in St. Marc has grown every year, and there are so many more children now compared to seven years ago when I first visited here. I wondered how they had survived the earthquake 2010 and what their lives were now like. When I got there, their smiles and joy were the same as I remembered from previous summers – they were just a year older and wiser!

Allie Dillon

THEY SURVIVED

I had just returned from Haiti, a day before the earthquake hit, just missing it. The epicenter of the 7.0 trembler was about 60 miles south of St. Marc. However, the earthquake and the after shocks were felt in St. Marc.

I was on the phone immediately after I heard about the earthquake and I spoke with people in St. Marc. There was panic. You could hear screaming in the background.

I was informed by phone that Good Samaritans School in St. Marc, Haiti, and the school children were "okay" after the devastating earthquake shook Haiti.

The following statement was released from the Mortel Family Charitable Foundation:

"As we are learning more about the devastating earthquake in Haiti, our hearts are bleeding. So many friends are suffering so much. Word from St. Marc is that the students of the Good Samaritans School are safe. The teachers kept the children calm in their classrooms and the building held up."

Dr. Rod Mortel

5

THE GLIMPSE OF HOPE STILL IN HAITI

As I approach Port-au-Prince, I notice the absence of traffic lights on the streets. Actually, it is not a street – just a dirt path. Little children are running in the streets having nowhere to go. I am shocked by the fact that these children have only the shirts on their backs and a tent over their heads. I feel grateful for what I have in America. The tents are a constant reminder – a reminder of the living hell these people experience every day. I think about the life I have and compare it to the lives of these children. Even though they have little, they seem appreciative for what they have.

As I arrive at Good Samaritans School, I am greeted by kind and welcoming smiles. I feel myself tingling inside. The children here are the poorest of the poor, but they do not act any differently than other kids. Their laughter echoes in my head like a choir singing on a stage. All around I see how their lives have been shattered by the 7.0 earthquake that changed their lives.

I smell the sewage that is running through the streets. It flows like a mountain spring, but instead of being pure, replenishing water, it carries diseases and germs. A young boy, no older than five, stands in the street with nothing on his body but a green shirt. He is flying a kite made out of a piece of string and part of a tent. Does he know there is more – more to life outside of Haiti? Will he ever escape his prison?

Hannah S. Patten

THE WOWS OF DR. MORTEL

Dr. Mortel is a huge inspiration to me. He is one of the kindest, most selfless, hard-working people I have ever met. If one man can start an organization that built two fantastic schools, feeding countless people everyday and educating the future of Haiti, imagine what would happen if everyone in the world worked to help one another.

"You are educated. Your certification is your degree. You may think of it as the ticket to the good life. Let me ask you to think of an alternative. Think of it as your ticket to change the world." – Tom Brokaw

Dr. Mortel used his education and extremely successful career as a "ticket" to change the world and make it a much better place. He has changed countless lives, including my own. I will never forget this amazing experience.

Lauren Kelly

9

THE CHANGES I SEE

I had the privilege of traveling to Haiti with my father, Dr. Mortel. It had been a number of years since my last trip and I was excited to visit both Good Samaritans School and James Stine College.

When I arrived in Haiti, I instantly noticed a number of changes in the country since my last visit.

As I traveled to St. Marc, I saw newly-populated areas which were the result of people migrating from the capital due to the earthquake. There were also new roads.

I couldn't believe how "westernized" St. Marc had become since I had last been there. Motorcycles and cars now flooded the streets that were once occupied by donkeys and bikes. The city now had an actual supermarket. The natives looked much more "American" in their clothing selection and hair styles. It seemed like everyone had a cell phone which made me smile as I remembered the times when you would have to go to a phone station to simply make a call to the United States.

Both of the schools were magnificent. Their structures spoke of greatness as I looked at how much they had progressed since I was last there. It was awesome to see the physical results of the countless donations received from our supporters. The number of students enrolled in each school was amazing. It was such a wonderful operation to witness. I was overwhelmed at how much had changed over the last decade.

But with that being said, I also noticed many things that were the same. Among them were: the spirit of the Haitian people; the big smiles on the children's faces; the warmth and love given by the student body when greeting me; the respect and discipline demonstrated in the classroom; the genuine laughter and happiness of the kids when interacting with Dr. Mortel; the sense of gratitude expressed by the principal, students and teachers for our visit. It was a humbling experience, one that I will never forget, and one that has further deepened my personal gratitude toward our many contributors for helping my father make this dream a reality for Haiti's "poorest of the poor."

Denise Mitchell

DANCING IS ROOTED IN HAITI

Dancing is a sacred treasure for Haitians. Dance has roots in the history of Haiti and it is something that is celebrated from birth. I recall growing up in Haiti and being taught that dancing was a form of expression. It is a way to share with others.

Students at Good Samaritans School and James Stine College are encouraged to join dance groups and many of the students practice routines before and after school when a big event is taking place. As I see the students dancing at ceremonies and special events, I am reminded of why I love Haiti so much.

Dr. Rod Mortel

I am thirteen years old, ister

I like the subject English.

I am the first black president of America

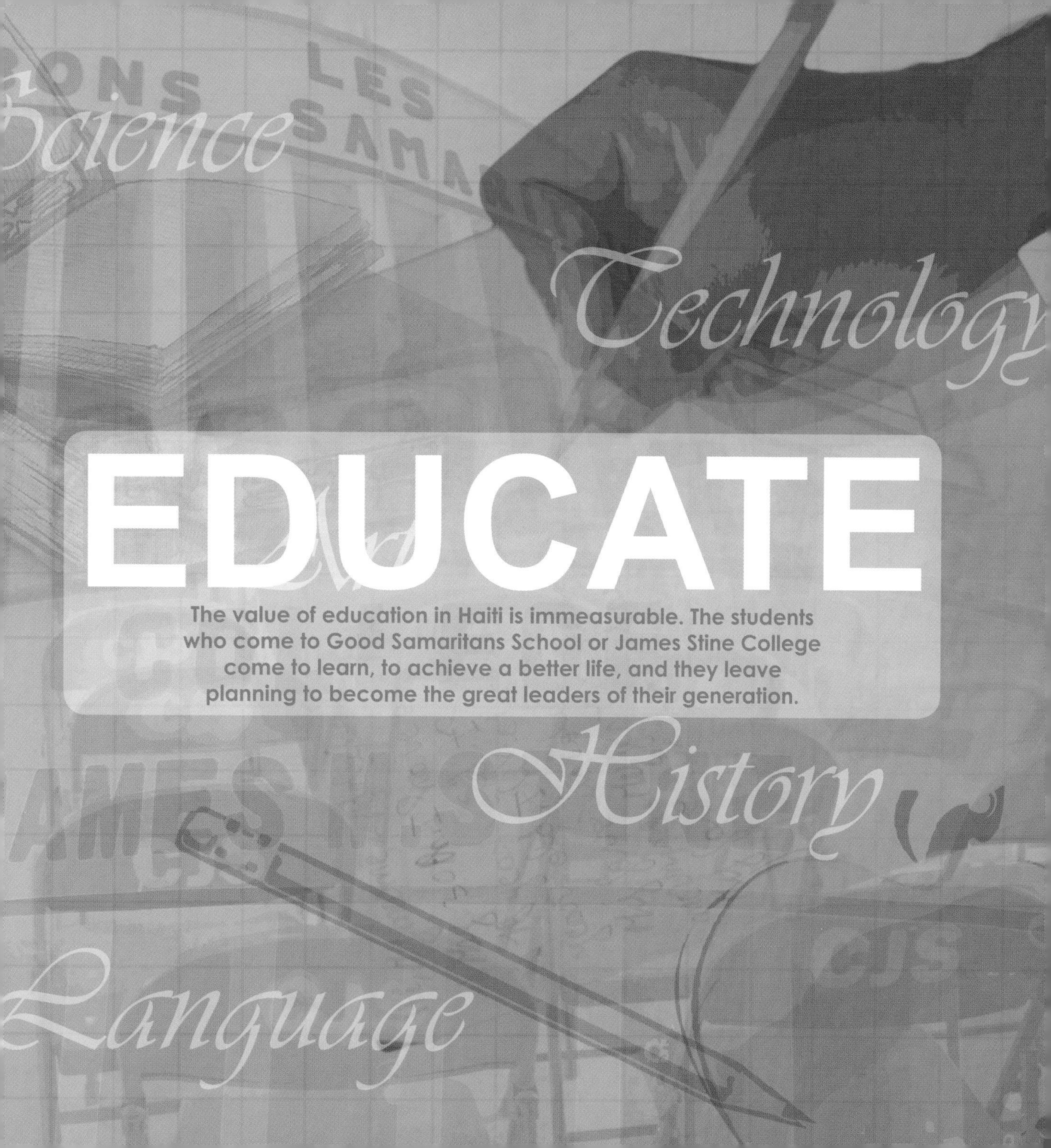

Science

LES SAMA

Technology

EDUCATE

The value of education in Haiti is immeasurable. The students who come to Good Samaritans School or James Stine College come to learn, to achieve a better life, and they leave planning to become the great leaders of their generation.

History

Language

EMPOWER THROUGH EDUCATION...

Good Samaritans School

The Good Samaritans School opened its wrought iron gate July 7, 2001, with a dedication ceremony and benediction by His Eminence, Cardinal William H. Keeler, archbishop of Baltimore. Contributions from Food for the Poor and private donors funded the construction of the three-story building.

Children enter the school at five years old, and are offered the opportunity for a free education through the sixth grade. They are given breakfast on arrival and a substantial meal following classes. In addition, all of the children in the school will undergo a yearly physical examination by a physician on site and a dental exam by volunteer dentists from the United States.

At the Good Samaritans School, 27 faculty members teach the students, under the direction of the Religious Congregation of St. Joseph de Cluny.

We have four kindergarten teachers and one teacher for each class first through sixth grade. For the seventh and eighth grades, instruction is carried out by specialized teachers for math, French, English, Spanish, science, music and computers. A teacher is assigned to the library and two additional teachers provide special assistance every afternoon to students who need academic help.

The support personnel are composed of two custodians and six workers in the kitchen. There are 45 employees paid 12 months a year and I am proud to report that we have virtually no staff turnover. With such a staff, the school has become the largest private employer in the city of St. Marc.

James Stine College

The James Stine College opened October 3, 2011, to welcome its first 270 students. The James Stine College offers quality secondary education to young women and men from the region and to those whose schools collapsed during the earthquake.

The Mortel Family Charitable Foundation board of directors entered into a 20-year contract with the Congregation of Clercs de St. Viateur, a religious congregation of priests and brothers, to direct James Stine College. The Montreal-based religious order began their responsibilities July 1, 2011.

The congregation will staff the principal position and will recruit the faculty and staff for the school. They also will serve as members of the school's administrative board.

The school serves students in 20 classrooms with the capacity to potentially reach 1,000 students.

PARTNERS IN GIVING

Thanks to UFCW's (United Food and Commercial Workers International Union) large donation, James Stine College will now have funds for the construction of a computer lab and library.

Jim Papin, UFCW communications director, said, "When the earthquake struck Haiti, so many United Food and Commercial Workers members generously donated money to international relief organizations that brought immediate relief like food, water, shelter and medical care. But the Haitian people still face a long road to recovery and the UFCW wanted to do something meaningful to help people recover in the long term. Our research indicated that education is the key to the country's recovery. The UFCW is proud to partner with the Mortel Family Charitable Foundation to support the building of a computer and library for James Stine College, a high school in St. Marc, Haiti. The school will provide quality secondary education to Haitian children from St. Marc and surrounding towns and parishes. Children today are leaders of tomorrow, and the UFCW wants to ensure that tomorrow's Haitian leaders are the best and brightest they can be."

Dr. Rod Mortel

> "Our research indicated that education is the key to the country's recovery."

BEACON OF HOPE

The school is so much more than the walls, desks and supplies. It is the most prestigious school in St. Marc; and its students are the brightest! I feel so lucky to be a part of such a wonderful academic setting – if only for a week!

There is no question that the students are Haiti's leaders of tomorrow. Words cannot capture their beautiful smiles or their spirit. It is sometimes hard for me to believe that they come from some of the poorest families in St. Marc, Haiti, because in their time spent at Good Samaritans School they have learned so much and demonstrated such potential.

The pillars for the school – belief in God, high standards of education, respect for each other, and love – are present and stronger than ever.

Judy Dillon

FUTURE LEADERS

After the sixth and ninth grade in Haiti, students are required to pass national exams. Because these tests are so important, students prepare for the test by taking practice tests and studying hard. The testing can be a stressful time for many students because the results determine if they continue on with their education.

For the past three years, 100 percent of our sixth grade students at Good Samaritans School have passed the first national exam.

Dr. Rod Mortel

ART IN ANY LANGUAGE...

My assignment was to do art projects with the students; ones that could be brought home to the Gala and sold to raise funds for the school. What I DIDN'T take into consideration was the fact that I didn't speak French and they didn't speak English!

Fortunately, art has the gift of bridging many gaps by its beauty and creativity (including communication gaps). The students were so gracious to give their art to us, understanding that it was for the school. I knew they would have loved to keep it for themselves!

Ellen Bundy

La Vie

Est Belle

 CONTINUING EDUCATION

A moment that we all hold dear to our hearts is school graduation. For me this year, I am especially proud of the sixth grade students who graduated from Good Samaritans School. I beamed with pride during the ceremony that included the graduates in red robes at the High Mass of Thanksgiving. These students will continue their education at the James Stine College.

Dr. Rod Mortel

24

JUST THE BEGINNING OF OUR JOURNEY

The grounds of James Stine College are equipped with everything the students or staff would need to provide the complete educational experience. There is a cafeteria, library, computer lab, bookstore, two chapels, science lab, multi-purpose room, medical and dental offices, offices for the receptionist and principal, a music room, volleyball and basketball courts and a soccer field.

Students at James Stine College gather in the school yard very early to raise the flag. At 7:30 a.m., the school bell rings and all classes line up by grade in the school yard.

All of the students then say the morning prayer. A designated class is assigned to lead the prayer each week and at the end, the principal adds special intentions.

Then the students enter their classrooms. They will stay in the same classroom during each lesson while teachers rotate. Every lesson is approximately one hour long with a mini-break for students at 9:30 a.m.

After lunch, classes continue until 3 p.m. for students. At this point in the day, the classical teaching portion is complete.

After-school activities then begin, like band practice and athletic team practice.

Dr. Rod Mortel

ACHIEVE

Good Samaritans School and James Stine College are institutions of learning, marked by the achievements of the students. The faces of the children tell a story of diligence and success.

CELEBRATION FOR A NATIVE SON

The church in St. Marc, Haiti, was overflowing with faithful who gathered on a sunny and warm morning to celebrate the ordination of Dr. Rod Mortel as a deacon.

Deacon Mortel grew up in this remote city about 50 miles north of Port-au-Prince. Today he was honored by well-wishers, family and friends who attended the religious service. The open doors to the church, which occasionally permitted a gentle breeze to circulate, were jammed with folks who couldn't get inside the crowded church.

Bishop Emmanuel Constant, bishop of Gonaives, the see city of the diocese that includes St. Marc, was the ordaining bishop.

Cardinal William H. Keeler, archbishop of Baltimore, was in attendance to support his good friend.

The liturgy was a festive three-hour celebration of song and prayer with frequent interruptions for sustained applause.

The new deacon preached his first homily in his native Creole and the congregation responded with enthusiasm.

Ordinations are always uplifting affairs. But this permanent diaconate ordination was a homecoming, a first for St. Marc, a thanksgiving and a blessing all in one.

Daniel Medinger

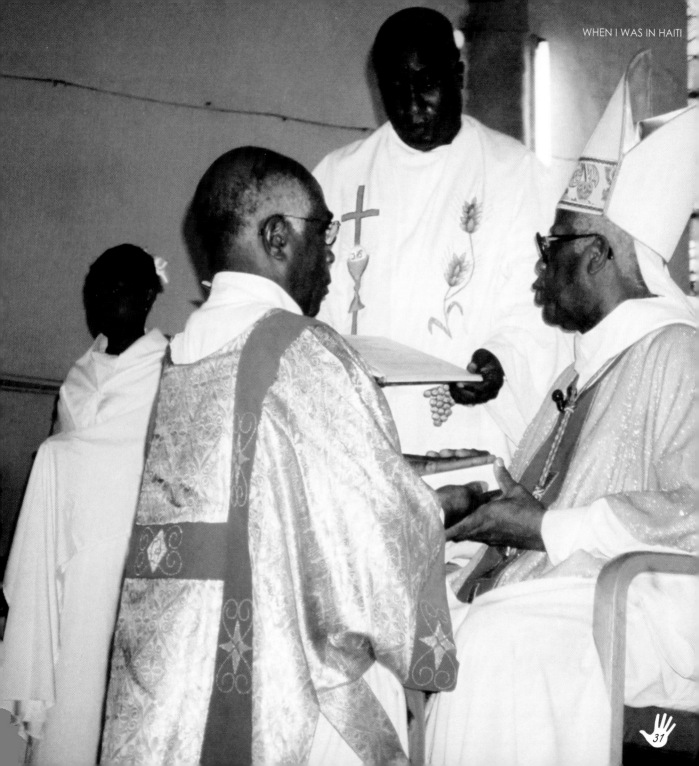

GOOD SAMARITANS SCHOOL AND CHANGING HISTORY

An historic event happened in St. Marc, Haiti. Good Samaritans School opened and it was a festive community celebration.

Dr. Rod Mortel, who founded the school, was beaming during the celebration which included singing, bands, speeches and tours of the gleaming new elementary school. Flags were hoisted and prayers were said. And one could only wonder what Dr. Mortel was thinking as he saw his dream of a school in his native city come to life?

Largely held in a sunny court yard, which is the entry way to the white brick and mortar building, the school's grand opening included an abundance of dignitaries from church, government and international aid organizations. Cardinal William H. Keeler, the archbishop of Baltimore who has supported and encouraged Dr. Mortel's vision to "empower through education," joined the celebration. Bishop Emmanuel Constant, who has worked side by side with Dr. Mortel in developing the educational program in this city of the Diocese of Gonaives, was also there smiling broadly.

As could be expected, there were speeches and proclamations. A large contingent from the Archdiocese of Baltimore and the Diocese of Harrisburg mixed with St. Marc residents.

But the real celebrities were the young boys and girls who are the first class at the new school. Dressed in their matching red and white checked school uniforms, they watched in wide-eyed amazement at the festivities. In the minds and hearts of these students is the future of Haiti.

For the students who were selected to receive "sponsored scholarships" to the school, admission to Good Samaritans School is like winning the lottery. An education, two meals a day, books and health care is a tremendous blessing for a child in Haiti.

In these children there is hope for the very future of this country. Today was a great day for a school opening. It also was the beginning of a new chapter in Haiti's history.

Daniel Medinger

UNBELIEVABLE – BUT IT IS TRUE

One of the most memorable occasions of my time spent in St. Marc was the kick off of the Jubilee year celebration. It was a gorgeous day and spirits were high. The students, teachers, principal and supporters all marched in the streets of St. Marc.

We sang the hymn of the school while the people of the city shared these joyous moments with us. The march was the beginning of a series of celebrations that honored the 10th year of Good Samaritans School.

Dr. Rod Mortel

AN UNFORGETTABLE MOMENT

I cannot possibly describe the scene following the Jubilee year celebration march through the streets of St. Marc, but I will try. After singing the school hymn repeatedly and with gusto for about an hour while marching through the streets, we ended up back in the school courtyard. When the Haitian National Anthem concluded, the children swarmed Dr. Mortel and literally swallowed him up. He disappeared into a sea of blue uniforms only to be raised up and carried, as if he were a feather, all around the school courtyard. It was a sight to behold and one I will never forget.

Willis Gunther

"**The bright confident smiles of these children, their love and gratefulness will forever be etched in my heart.**"

HOW FAR WE'VE COME

I am often asked the question in a seemingly negative tone, "How are things in Haiti?" The challenge and excitement to describe the progress I have seen over the past 10 years, particularly since the inception of Good Samaritans School in St. Marc, has been overwhelming. So much has been accomplished since the land was purchased in 1996 and the architectural drawings were complete.

In 2001, the school was dedicated, opening its doors to 65 needy kindergarten children. In 2003, a four bedroom residence to house volunteers was completed and in 2004, a third floor, with an additional eight classrooms, was added to accommodate an average of 600 underprivileged students from kindergarten through sixth grade. Five years later, additional land, adjacent to the school building, was purchased to increase the surface of the school yard. Two years ago, in 2010 the construction of the secondary school began and in September, 2011, the first 270 students were welcomed at James Stine College. All of this has been phenomenal.

Even more remarkable has been the progress of the students over the past 10 years. Each year their excitement for their education is progressively evident, their compassion, with a sense of purpose, increasingly palpable and their determination to reach their full potential becomes unmistakable. The bright confident smiles of these children, their love and gratefulness will forever be etched in my heart.

Yes, over the last 10 years much has been accomplished in St. Marc by the grace of God, the focused leadership of Dr. Mortel, the tireless work of many volunteers and the generosity of hundreds of donors from the United States, Germany, France and Italy. May this wonderful and fruitful journey continue to prepare these children to become the future leaders of Haiti.

Cecile Mortel

COLLEGE
JAMES M.STINE

IT'S COMPLETE

It has been a long journey, but with every good journey the end result is far greater than one could imagine. James Stine College is complete!

When students complete the curriculum at James Stine College after seven years, they will be ready to enter medical school, law school, and other graduate programs and technical schools.

Dr. Rod Mortel

A TIME TO CELEBRATE

The James Stine College dedication on January 29, 2012, was nothing less than celebrating the glory and power of God.

A group of 46 travelers spent four days in Haiti witnessing the beauty of the country and the success of the schools that we have built over the past 11 years.

The pilgrimage started when the travelers arrived in St. Marc, Haiti. They received the warmest welcome. Students at Good Samaritans School stood in the courtyard singing a welcome song in English for the travelers. I could see that the love the students immediately showed put a smile on everyone's face.

Dr. Rod Mortel

KEEPING OUR STUDENTS SAFE

A huge improvement has been made to both the Good Samaritans School and the James Stine College. Thanks to "International Action," an organization based in Washington, D.C., each school received a 2,000 gallon water purification system.

This drinking water system (dlo pwop in Creole) was donated and installed by a team of technicians from that organization, making Good Samaritans School and James Stine College the only schools in St. Marc, Haiti, with the capability of providing purified water on a large scale, and free of charge.

This chlorinated water has the potential to kill germs of all waterborne diseases such as cholera, typhoid, hepatitis, and so on. This is another step taken to keep our children safe. It is our intention to make this water available also to all individuals living in the vicinity.

Dr. Rod Mortel

FAITH

Faith is believing in things unseen. Travelers to Haiti witness the tremendous faith that provides the strength to overcome a legacy of challenges. Daily life in Haiti is filled with expressions of belief and trust in God.

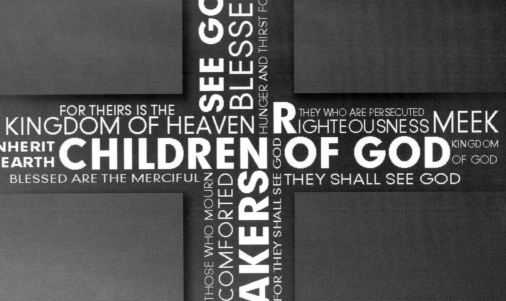

I NEEDED TO KNOW HIS NAME

When Aristotle said that humans learn through sensible experience, I think he was on to something.

For me, I needed to know his name, to see his smile; I needed to watch him play soccer and to referee between friends over whether or not the shot was a goal. He was Rominigue, a fifth grader at Good Samaritans School, and it definitely was not a goal. And the smile? It made his eyes dance and gave off a mischievous smirk that made you wonder what he wasn't saying.

At first glance it seems Rominigue and I have almost nothing in common. The color of our skin and the language we speak is the least of our differences. Yet in one week he was able to powerfully draw me in to the sorrows and burdens of his young life.

If you look hard enough, though, you might be able to detect in Rominigue's eyes something which is very different from what we found in so many other eyes we met in that town. Rominigue's eyes give a joyful spark, a glimmer of hope. In a country so overcome by despair, the students within the haven of Good Samaritans School are receiving a gift that has the power to overcome even the most desperate situations. Rominigue, like his many school mates, knows that someone believes in his ability to succeed and more importantly, he knows his dignity and the value of his life.

Abby Hill

PREPARING FOR GOD

It has been a privilege and a gift for me to go to Haiti every year for the last four years to baptize children at Good Samaritans School in St. Marc.

These baptisms follow two years of sacramental preparation. The baptism is preceded by a spiritual retreat of one-week duration.

In the public ceremony, after they have been baptized, the children express the hope that other children and adults will follow their example. I am impressed that these children are so well aware of what they are doing and what it means to be baptized.

Dr. Rod Mortel

ⓜ ENTERING INTO THE FAITH

For years, many parents of Good Samaritans School students have expressed the desire to have their child enter the Catholic faith. These children receive a two-year preparation before being baptized and then one more year before their first communion.

Once completed, a High Mass with liturgical dances is held in the courtyard of Good Samaritans School to celebrate. An open invitation and reception is shared with the students' parents to witness this big day.

The day is compared to a wedding for the family. The family will save money for this special event and host an "open house" for all relatives and friends to celebrate.

I'm thankful I was able, as a deacon, to assist the main celebrant and be a part of this extremely special moment. I was happy to share it with the students, staff, parents, supporters and my clerical colleagues.

I thank God every day for allowing the school to continue to preach the gospel of Jesus Christ.

Dr. Rod Mortel

THE HAITIAN WAY

The Haitian people truly understand that everyone is a child of God, and therefore they treat everyone as God. The unhesitating giving and caring of the Haitians struck me because they had so little themselves. Hopefully people everywhere can begin to adopt the Haitian spirit and willingness to serve others as a small step to helping the world.

I did not know Creole when we landed in Haiti, but we did not need to know it to be able to communicate with the students. A simple smile or hand gesture was enough. While sweeping one day, we found that many of the kids knew the same songs we did, and we spent hours singing and working together. That was one of the best experiences I have ever had. When we went to Mass in Haiti, we did not need to know the language to follow the Mass. Receiving Christ in Haiti is the same as receiving Christ in the United States. God is universal.

Dignity was a theme that our group talked about frequently throughout the week, and one that the Haitians understand. We should be in awe of human life. We should treat others with respect and care less about ourselves.

Laura Goudreau

MANY BLESSINGS

I thank God every day for allowing the school to be a success and I also thank our benefactors who continue to support our effort. The Jubilee Mass was our best way to pray for all of them.

I was able to participate in the liturgy as a deacon assisting the main celebrant who is the provincial superior of the religious congregation that directs our high school. In all, 16 priests concelebrated.

Many students and parents participated. Students and teachers decorated the courtyard with ribbons and flowers to prepare for the week-long celebration.

Dr. Rod Mortel

HOPE

With so much beauty, Haiti is a place of hope. Through their selfless spirits, the children of Haiti share a ray of hope with every life they touch.

A PRAYER FOR HAITI

As I stand here under the Haitian night sky writing this reflection, I already feel overwhelmed by my brief stay. Haiti is a beautiful country; God's love is very much alive here and, with prayers and investment, this country will soar in every way possible. There is so much hope for Haiti. I have seen hope in every child that came to the camp that I was blessed enough to help run. The children have drive, talent and an optimistic outlook for their futures. The students, by the grace of God, will allow Haiti to achieve its full potential.

I leave Haiti with higher hopes and a deeper love. If faith is truly the combination of hope and love, then my faith has intensified. God bless Haiti. May God guide Haiti, and may those who can, use their God-given gifts to fulfill the hopes and dreams of God's children in this beautiful nation.

Anebi Adoga, Jr.

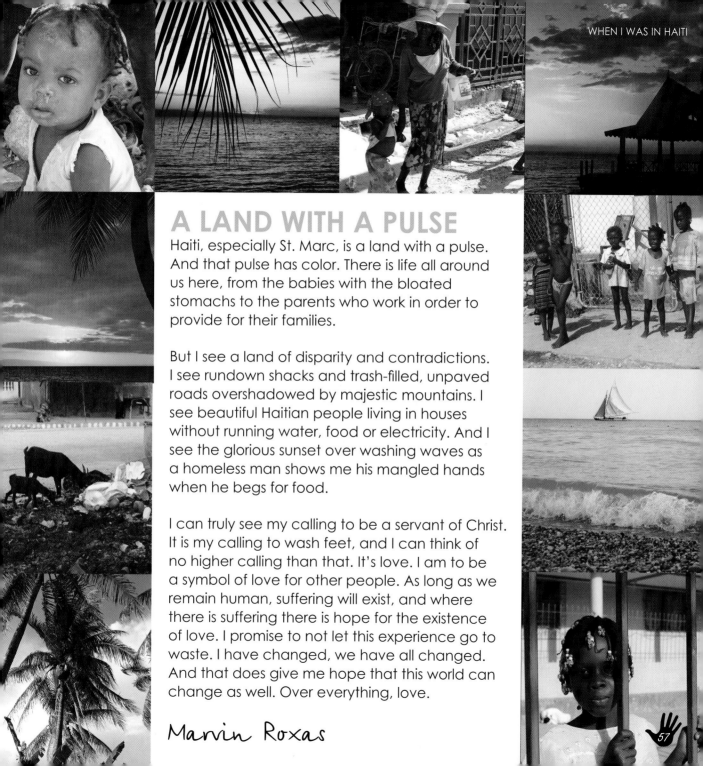

A LAND WITH A PULSE

Haiti, especially St. Marc, is a land with a pulse. And that pulse has color. There is life all around us here, from the babies with the bloated stomachs to the parents who work in order to provide for their families.

But I see a land of disparity and contradictions. I see rundown shacks and trash-filled, unpaved roads overshadowed by majestic mountains. I see beautiful Haitian people living in houses without running water, food or electricity. And I see the glorious sunset over washing waves as a homeless man shows me his mangled hands when he begs for food.

I can truly see my calling to be a servant of Christ. It is my calling to wash feet, and I can think of no higher calling than that. It's love. I am to be a symbol of love for other people. As long as we remain human, suffering will exist, and where there is suffering there is hope for the existence of love. I promise to not let this experience go to waste. I have changed, we have all changed. And that does give me hope that this world can change as well. Over everything, love.

Marvin Roxas

SHARE ALL THAT YOU ARE

So often since our return from Haiti, I have been asked, "So, how was it?" Without hesitation, with a tear in my eye and a tug at my heart, my genuine enthusiastic response is, "It was the best experience I have ever had in my life," since the birth of our children.

Through my eyes, in my heart, in laughter, silence and in the many embraces with Adeline, Dieula, Nancy, Dinah, Merites, Wilson, Maxie, Bene, Bedia and Tammy – they have all taught me what it is to be rich in the meaning and purpose of life – simply by being who they are.

It is obvious that the people of Haiti taught us how to share all that you are and all that you have, even if it means a personal sacrifice – our challenge is to look at our own life and respond from our heart with the same selfless spirit of generosity and compassion with the gifts that we have been given.

Kathy Mayer

HAITI CHANGES YOU

I have participated in numerous dress-down days, fundraisers and food drives at Archbishop Spalding High School. I have been intrigued and inspired to help because of the speeches and slide shows by Mr. Patrick Brady. However, at no point over the past three years have I ever felt the utter connection and deep understanding of Haiti as I do now, after spending a week in the country.

All the awareness effort at home is impressive and definitely effective, but a mere six days of my life spent in Haiti has changed me forever.

I have gained a hero in Dr. Mortel, who is hands-down the most fascinating and inspiring person I have ever had the honor of meeting. My week in Haiti was all about giving everything I could to this country in need, but in looking back on it, I must acknowledge that the knowledge and experience I have gained is invaluable. This trip was truly unforgettable and life-changing. It is something that I pray to be able to do again and that I believe everyone should have the opportunity to do.

Becca Dean

MAKING FRIENDS

The children of Good Samaritans School, the poorest of the poor, people with virtually nothing, have so much more love, happiness and joy than I could ever hope to have. Luckily for me, I had the honor and privilege of meeting these wonderful people and they have helped me see what is truly important.

Little Benadiane taught me to see the importance of brightening everyone's day. With the warmth of her little smile, my day was made and happiness truly did fill my heart.

Adeline taught me to always have the strength to face life. Despite the adversity she has been through – so much pain and suffering – she still finds the passion in life and loves everyone with ferocity and brings so much joy to the room when she enters.

I won't soon forget Kenny and the excitement we shared when our team won a game of basketball. That little boy will warm my heart forever.

I have a new found friend named Tamara, who taught me cultural borders can be broken down to form friendships that will last a lifetime.

We have a duty to help our brothers and sisters who are struggling. My trip to Haiti ignited fire and passion in me and I hope everyone finds this passion one day, too.

Danielle Freiji

GIVING

Life is a gift, and it offers the privilege, opportunity and responsibility to give something back.

"They have lost everything but their life."

OPEN DOORS...OPEN HEARTS

After the earthquake, 65 students were recently admitted to Good Samaritans School after they migrated from Port-au-Prince to St. Marc. You cannot fully appreciate what these children and parents have been through since the earthquake devastated the Haiti capital. The best way that I can express it is this: they have lost everything but their life.

I am pleased that we had spaces in the school to admit these 65 students. The normal routine of the classroom environment will help them as they cope with the dramatic changes in their lives. The children are meeting with a clinical psychologist to help them overcome the trauma. Their parents, too, are adjusting to a life that only a few months ago they could not imagine.

Dr. Rod Mortel

NEVER TOO POOR TO GIVE

The children at Good Samaritans School never cease to amaze me. Under the direction of the faculty, the students are learning values along with their academic studies.

During Advent and Lent, the children every day bring in a few pennies, whatever they can find. The money collected is used to purchase, cook and deliver a meal to the 317 prisoners in the St. Marc jail.

I am so proud of these children. I am also proud of those who teach them to be generous. These children are proof that one is never too poor to be able to give.

Dr. Rod Mortel

EDUCATION FOR SERVICE

"Officers eat last," was the message Cardinal Edwin O'Brien gave to James Stine College students and the people of St. Marc at the dedication.

He told a heartfelt story from his military years about putting others first to be successful. Cardinal O'Brien's speech inspired the students to use their education for service.

From the very beginning, Cardinal O'Brien supported our mission in Haiti. He deserves a special thank you.

Just as Cardinal O'Brien said during his homily, "We plant the seed, God does the rest."

Dr. Rod Mortel

AS LONG AS GOD ALLOWS ME

God gives us each special gifts to share and these gifts can be used for remarkable things.

Tim Lear led a team of carpenters from parishes in Pennsylvania and Maryland who traveled to Haiti to share their skills. The group consisted of John Lear, Bill Lear, Richard Ulrich, Joe Phebus, Brian Crook, Larry Duckart, John Moyer and Isaac Moyer.

Tim Lear does immeasurable things with his gifts. He told me, "I have become very attached to some of the children of the school. John and I have known some of them since the year the school opened in 2001. What a joy it has been to work in Haiti over the years. I will continue to work as long as God allows me to."

But, for another crew member, Richard Ulrich, this was his first time in Haiti. He was prepared for the poverty in Haiti because of his volunteer work in Nicaragua, but he was not prepared for the dedication of the Haitian work crew also working on the school. He told me, "They mixed the concrete on the ground and then formed an assembly line to pass bucket by bucket up to the roof. Here in the United States a truck would have been delivered with mixed concrete and then a pump would have been used to reach the roof."

Dr. Rod Mortel

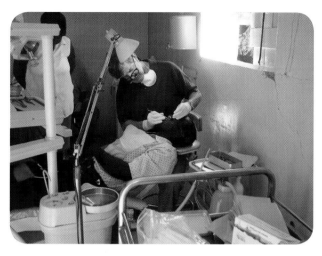

 # HEALTHY SMILES...

As part of our health program, dental care and treatment are provided to our students. Once a year a team of dentists volunteers their time to the children of Good Samaritans School. During those couple of days the children are reminded of the importance of dental hygiene. This is one of my highlights because education is extending beyond the traditional subjects.

Once they were out of the dentist chair, each child received a tooth brush and toothpaste to continue to practice dental hygiene.

It is truly a blessing when you see the sun shine off of their white smiles.

Dr. Rod Mortel

> ## "It is truly a blessing when you see the sun shine off of their white smiles."

IT HAS ARRIVED!
Can you believe it?

It has been 10 years since the Good Samaritans School building was complete and ready to open its doors to the first class of students.

The theme of the year will be "Thank You" to acknowledge the supporters who have followed us for this first decade. The success of Good Samaritans School would not have been possible without you!

Dr. Rod Mortel

On the next page is a speech on behalf of all parents of the Good Samaritans School's graduating class of 2012, made by Mrs. Leonce Joseph, mother of student Emula Joseph.

A PARENT SAYS THANK YOU

Except for family, school is the oldest institution, the social group the most indispensable to mankind. It is the epicenter of education and the extension of the family unit. In other words, school is a mandatory step in life.

Indeed the literacy level of a nation is an indication of that nation's values. Consequently as parents, we claim that, likewise, a society is as good as the value it gives to education.

Teachers, you are the roots and the pillars of the society, the backbone of education. Your dedication and commitment are essential for the success of any institutional program. Fortunately the educational activities in this institution are coordinated by the tireless Sister Marie Bernard. Felicitations, sister. Please keep up the good work.

Dr. Rodrigue Mortel, the founder, the man with the vision, we have not found words strong enough to thank you and express our gratitude. But in His infinite love, the Lord will save a special place for you in His kingdom. You have achieved what no one before you could accomplish in this city of Nissage Sajet. Indeed, without you, the school "Les Bons Samaritains" would remain a dream, a utopia. But thanks to your dynamism and your administrative ability, our school has become what it is today, a school of reference where the fundamental right to education and health care as well as the need to feed the children are respected and carried out. In our school nothing is missing.

As far as James Stine College is concerned, what can we say? Even those negative individuals who criticize everything in this city have testified to the significance of this master piece. Therefore, Dr. Mortel, the words which could express our gratitude are hidden at the bottom of our hearts.

For us, you represent a monument. For our children, you are a special grandfather, the best role model and an instrument of social progress. For the city of St. Marc you are a visionary and a sociocultural heritage. Yes, Dr. Mortel, your actions will follow you and will make of you an immortal Dr. Mortel. THANK YOU.

Mrs. Leonce D. Joseph   *Translation from French to English by Mr. Philippe Jallon*

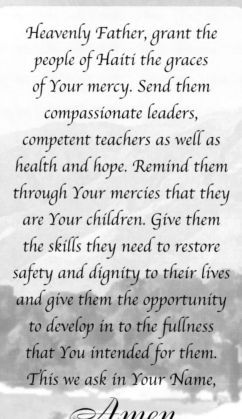

Heavenly Father, grant the
people of Haiti the graces
of Your mercy. Send them
compassionate leaders,
competent teachers as well as
health and hope. Remind them
through Your mercies that they
are Your children. Give them
the skills they need to restore
safety and dignity to their lives
and give them the opportunity
to develop in to the fullness
that You intended for them.
This we ask in Your Name,

Amen

AFTERWORD

Go there.

This book is all about going there. Whether it's Dr. Mortel or other travelers, "When I was in Haiti" tells the story of what happens when someone from here goes there.

Part of that story is the reaction that people have about going to Haiti. In fact, "go there" can take on an entirely different meaning by how the words are emphasized. Go there can be a statement of fact when said evenly. Go there. It also can be a question of incredulity: Go there? Or it can be an exclamation of commitment: Go there!

Travelers who have written for this book, many of whom also contributed touching photographs, all confess to being changed by the experience of going to Haiti, meeting the students and seeing how the Mortel Family Charitable Foundation is "empowering through education."

Travelers say that their pre-conceived notions about Haiti were changed by being there. They are charmed by the beauty of a land that's often characterized by the clichés of poverty. They are inspired by the faith and hope of the people. They are captivated by the "joie de vivre" that Haitians bring to every day experiences.

After going there, travelers come back with a deeper question about what it means to be poor. Yes, there is material poverty in Haiti, but they are rich in spirit. The travelers wonder how material richness may also create poverty of the spirit here.

"When I was in Haiti" is a series of narratives about how givers (those who travel there) also become receivers. This book is about how the students at Good Samaritans School and James Stine College are receiving an opportunity for a better life and how they are giving back by inspiring those who visit them.

A little more than 10 years ago, Dr. Mortel, Cardinal William H. Keeler and Bishop Emmanuel Constant (then bishop of the Diocese of Gonaives) dreamed of building two schools in St. Marc, Haiti. At that time, could anyone predict that there would be two flourishing schools in this Haitian port city? Dr. Mortel has provided the vision, the leadership and the energy. He has been supported by many (hopefully you are one of them) and the dream has become a reality that exceeds anyone's expectations.

Looking back over the last decade, God's hand has been at work in helping the schools emerge, grow and succeed. Looking forward, what is the future of the schools and the students? Well, if God is on your side you know how the story will go. And if you want to know for yourself, you should plan to "go there."